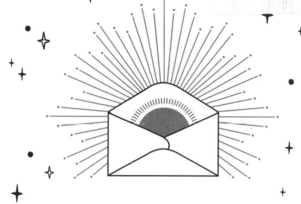

LETTERS
TO THE
Universe

50 Guided Letters to Help You Script and Manifest the Life You Want

KELSEY AIDA ROUALDES

◆ ——— ◆
ADAMS MEDIA
New York ◆ London ◆ Toronto ◆ Sydney ◆ New Delhi

*For everyone who's listening to their
heart and going for their dreams.*

Adams Media
An Imprint of Simon & Schuster, Inc.
100 Technology Center Drive
Stoughton, Massachusetts 02072

First Adams Media trade paperback
edition January 2022

ADAMS MEDIA and colophon are
trademarks of Simon & Schuster.

For information about special
discounts for bulk purchases, please
contact Simon & Schuster Special
Sales at 1-866-506-1949 or business@
simonandschuster.com.

The Simon & Schuster Speakers Bureau
can bring authors to your live event. For
more information or to book an event
contact the Simon & Schuster Speakers
Bureau at 1-866-248-3049 or visit our
website at www.simonspeakers.com.

Interior design, illustrations, and hand
lettering by Priscilla Yuen
Interior images © 123RF/Gemma Hester,
Kseniya Dziusmikeyeva, mykate,
nikoniano

Manufactured in the United States of
America

1 2021

ISBN 978-1-5072-1808-2

CONTENTS

—

INTRODUCTION

Welcome to *Letters to the Universe*—your interactive guide to manifesting your dreams through the magic of writing! Writing is one of the most powerful, fun, and effective ways to state your intentions and set your goals in motion. Not only does it give the Universe a clear picture of what you want to experience next, but it also helps *you* start lining up with your desires mentally and emotionally, building powerful, energetic momentum. When you write things out the good old-fashioned way, you create a direct line of communication to your subconscious mind, a key player in the manifestation process. With every word, you are literally programming yourself for victory.

In Part 1 of this book, you'll explore manifestation in more depth. Here you'll learn what the full process of manifestation between you and the Universe looks like, and what your role in manifesting your goals involves. This part will also help you get into the right headspace for effective manifesting by offering tips for increasing your chances of succeeding, as well as insights into what you'll want to avoid when trying to manifest.

Part 2 is where things get interactive, as you start scripting your future by getting clear on what you want and then deliberately communicating it to the Universe via a handwritten letter! Each letter comes with a brainstorming section to help you gain insight and get ready to manifest. Use these questions to conduct a curiosity-driven self-inquiry into what you want. The better you understand your desire, yourself, and any potential energetic blockages, the easier it will be for you to manifest!

Once you've spent some time brainstorming, take what you've learned and include it in your letter to the Universe. Use the template following each brainstorming session to write about your desire and thank the Universe for the gifts you're about to receive. You can write your letter in the present tense, as if you are already living your fulfilled wish. Or you can write your letter about the future and how excited you are to experience what you want. There is no right or wrong when it comes to what you include in your letter, so don't feel like you have to incorporate *all* of your answers from the brainstorming session. Just write from the heart about what you want to manifest, creating a vivid picture in your mind as you do. The more descriptive you are, especially about how you want to *feel*, the better. See, feel, hear, smell, and even taste your creations in your mind before they have arrived. This will prime you to receive!

When your letter is done, be creative with what you do with it next. You can post it somewhere to look at every day as a reminder of what's to come, tuck it away in a dream box to "set it and forget it," or even get together with friends or family so you can each write a letter and then (safely) burn them to symbolize releasing your desires to the Universe. Whatever you do with your letter, have fun and get excited: Your dreams are closer than you think!

PART 1

How to Manifest

WHAT IS MANIFESTATION?

As a living, breathing part of this ever-expanding Universe, you possess the same creative abilities that It does. Think of the Universe as the macro and yourself as the micro. If the Universe were the ocean, you would be a water droplet in it—a part of the whole that's made up of the same exact elements and has the same distinct qualities. One of the cooler traits you have in common with the Universe is the ability to create something from nothing and turn thoughts into things—a.k.a. the ability to manifest!

Whether you realize it or not, most manifesting is as natural and involuntary for you as breathing, and you've already been doing it! Life brings about diverse experiences, which lead you to specific desires, which eventually cause you to create/manifest new experiences. Manifesting *intentionally*, however, as you will be doing with the help of this journal, refers to the act of *consciously* co-creating with the Universe. It entails becoming aware of your desires, opening up a dialogue about them, and then lining yourself up with them both energetically and physically. You can manifest all sorts of things, from better overall circumstances or a dream job you've always wanted, to a beautiful partnership, an improved emotional state, or even just a great parking spot at the grocery store.

The manifesting process works like this:

+ **STEP ZERO:** This is the prep work that occurs naturally. You gain life experience (wanted and unwanted) that causes you to ask for new or improved experiences. The contrast between your experiences and your desires helps you to give birth to certain wants.

+ **STEP ONE:** You'll use the information you gathered from step zero to set an intention for your life. This is your time to claim your desires! You can do so in the form of a request (something that you ask for) or a declaration (something that you state belongs to your future self). However you frame it, as soon as you know what you want, so does the

Universe. Now the magic starts to happen and energies begin to move in your favor, which leads to step two.

+ **STEP TWO:** This is when the Universe responds, and It always responds with a yes! There's nothing for you to do in this step besides sit back, relax, and trust that things are starting to come together behind the scenes. People, things, opportunities, and circumstances are being rearranged and repurposed on your behalf. Remember that the Universe has every single possible resource at Its disposal.

+ **STEP THREE:** This step involves a little more work on your part. Here you'll start to take inspired action, make empowering changes to your life, and do some healing work or mindset tweaks to prepare for the arrival of your manifestation! After all, the version of you that has what you want isn't the same version you are today. A big part of the manifesting process is the personal development that takes place between the asking and receiving. Because in order to receive what you want, you must first be a vibrational match for it. Step three is where you make yourself a match if you aren't one already. (More on how to do this later.)

+ **STEP FOUR:** This is the moment you've been waiting for...you get to receive! You've asked, you've aligned yourself energetically, and now you're ready to enjoy the fruits of your request.

No matter how little or big a desired outcome may seem, with the right intention, focus, and lack of resistance, it can happen!

IDENTIFYING WHAT YOU WANT

The first part of step one in the manifestation process is to identify what it is that you want. It sounds pretty simple, but you would be surprised how many people don't actually know! The key is to become consciously aware of your desire so you can give the Universe some clear direction to help you out. It's pretty hard to create what you want when you don't even know what it *really* is, so this part is crucial.

You probably already have some idea of what you want since you are reading this book, but if you're having trouble pinning it down, the fastest way to find out what you want is, ironically, to notice what you *don't* want. By looking at the contrast of your life (meaning the circumstances or moments that cause you pain or suffering), you can figure out what the opposite of those experiences would be and uncover your desire! When you're feeling sad, you want happiness. When you're in financial trouble, you want more money. When you're alone, you want connection and community.

Once you have realized what you want, it's important to take it a step further and ask yourself *why*. Why do you want it? How do you think you will *feel* different when you have it? In other words, what core feeling(s) are you looking for? Maybe you want to lose weight so you can feel lighter and healthier. Maybe you want a dog so you can experience unconditional love and loyal companionship. Maybe you want millions of dollars so you can have total freedom and the financial resources to do whatever you want, whenever you want!

The real reason why you want anything in life is because you think you will feel different (better) in having it. This makes perfect sense, because it's sometimes true (and sometimes not). This is why it's helpful to think through your desires carefully before you go about creating them. You may have thought you wanted one thing, but upon deeper questioning, you realize that you want something totally different. And that's okay! That's what this process is for: self-exploration and creative expression. Making sure you *do* want what you think you want is extremely empowering, because it will give you the clarity you need to go after your desires in the most direct and efficient way.

When you fully understand why you want what you want, you will not only have more clarity and direction; you'll also have the "cheat code" to help you manifest it faster. The core feeling(s) that you're after isn't just a potential by-product of receiving your manifestation; it's also the fastest way for you to line up with your manifestation energetically. (You'll learn more about this in a later section.)

ASKING THE UNIVERSE FOR HELP

Life is made up of relationships. You relate to your partner, your friends, your family, your coworkers, your neighbors, your in-laws, your pets, yourself…but you also relate to non-people things like your work, your home, your car, your phone, your emotions, social media, food, nature, this journal, and the Universe! In all relationships, the healthier the connection is, the more pleasurable it feels, and the more value it adds to your life. This journal will help you improve a few important ones—your relationship with desire, your relationship with yourself, your relationship with the Universe, and your relationship with life itself.

When relating to the Universe, it's helpful to imagine that the Universe is like a person. Like you, this "person" has feelings, needs, desires, preferences—a personality! One thing you should understand about this "person" is that they are *always* on your side (even when it doesn't feel like it), and they want what you want. You can think of the Universe as an unconditionally supportive friend—always cheering you on, trying to help in any way they can!

The important thing is to *let* the Universe help you. Remember steps one and two in the manifestation process? You have to know your intention and realize that the Universe can and will help you experience it. This will require some communication, openness, and trust on your end. After all, how can someone help you if you don't ask or allow them to?

The good news is, just by existing on this planet, you are "asking" all the time, through your preferences and desires. And while you don't need to vocalize them for the Universe to know what you want and need, it is helpful to do so for a few reasons:

1. It helps *you* become more aware of what you want so that you will know it when you see it.

2. It helps create energetic momentum to talk about and/or write about what you want. (In other words, the more time you spend focused on what you want, the more creative energy starts to build and move in your favor.)

3. It's a fun way to manifest and improve your relationship with the Universe!

In this journal, you will be using writing as the primary form of asking for/declaring what you want, but you can also say your desires out loud for emphasis.

RAISING YOUR VIBRATION

Let's talk about your vibe, a.k.a. your vibration: the key to step three of the manifestation process. At any given moment, your energy is vibrating at a certain frequency. In other words, your consciousness is either more closed and restrictive or more open, aware, and unconditionally loving. The higher your consciousness, the higher your vibration, and vice versa. Your frequency and your consciousness go hand in hand.

The easiest way to gauge your vibration is simply by noticing how you feel. Your emotions will always tell you where you are vibrationally because they are literally energy in motion (e-motion!). You can tell you're in a high-vibrational state when you're feeling things like love, gratitude, happiness, excitement, peace, passion, and other positive emotions. These fast-moving frequencies make you a magnet for manifesting! On the contrary, you can tell you're in a low-vibrational state when you feel things like depression, loneliness, hatred, jealousy, disgust, fear, and so on. These slower, denser energies are opportunities to tend to yourself and your needs until you naturally return to a higher vibrational state.

In a perfect world, we would all feel great all the time and would always be in a high-vibrational state of alignment. But this just isn't how human beings operate. That's okay, because both higher (expansive) and lower (contractive) vibrational states have value in the manifesting process. When you're in a low-vibrational state, you birth strong desires to feel better and experience the opposite of whatever has caused you unhappiness. This sets manifestation into motion! When you're feeling down is not the best time to do fun manifestation work such as writing letters to the Universe, but it is a great time to conduct some compassionate self-inquiry to figure out what personal truth your negative feeling is trying to point out to you. This clarity will ultimately help you get to where you want to go. So it's not all bad!

When you're in a high-vibrational state, you become a match to what you have asked for in the past, meaning you are primed and prepped to receive! Because the whole premise of the Law of Attraction is that like energy attracts like energy—when you're in a feel-good state you are an energetic match to feel-good experiences. This is the best time to do fun intention-setting work such as writing your letters.

To raise your vibrational state, start by familiarizing yourself with your thoughts, and then get selective about which ones you choose to entertain and subscribe to. Because your thoughts affect how you feel, and how you feel is a gauge for your vibrational state, the better a thought makes you feel, the more high-vibrational it is. The worse a thought makes you feel, the more low-vibrational it is. Consciously choosing thoughts that help you feel good, or at least better, is how you can consistently raise your vibrational state on a momentary and daily basis.

There are many other efficient practices, exercises, and positive mindset tools available to help you cultivate a higher vibrational state every day. One of the easiest ways to climb up the vibrational scale when you're not feeling super positive is to practice radical authenticity and nonresistance with your emotions. This means getting real about how you feel and not resisting or judging it, so as to let it pass more quickly. A lot of teachings emphasize that feeling good is the key to manifesting, but it's much more accurate to say that being good *at* feeling is the key. Don't use your spiritual knowledge against yourself and insist that you "stay positive" for the sake of being "high-vibe." Accepting that you came here to feel it *all* and remembering that feeling "bad" doesn't have to mean anything negative about you or your life is extremely helpful in these moments. It's when you make feeling bad *mean* that something is wrong with you or your life that you suffer unnecessarily and put yourself in a state of resistance, which is not conducive to manifesting what you want. The less you hold on to resistance, the more you can go with the flow and naturally line up with your highest vibrational self with little effort, especially after an undesirable emotional experience.

EXPLORING THE DOS AND DON'TS OF MANIFESTING

Certain practices can transform even the most defeating manifesting struggles into manifesting successes quite quickly. The following are helpful guidelines to follow throughout your manifesting journey. Stick to these dos and don'ts, and you'll be a manifesting pro in no time!

✳ DO KEEP IT FUN

Manifesting works best when it's fun and playful. Any intention-setting exercise will be the most beneficial when it's sponsored by the energies of creativity and imagination. So keep it light, have fun with it, and don't take yourself too seriously.

✳ DO WRITE WHEN YOU'RE FEELING INSPIRED

The best time to write a letter to the Universe is when you're feeling inspired and in alignment! This could be right after a great workout at the gym, while you're enjoying some sun on a tropical beach, or simply right before bedtime as you let your mind imagine the possibilities of the future. You'll know when the time is right for you.

✳ DO STAY FLEXIBLE

It's your job to let the Universe know *what* you want, and it's the Universe's job to figure out the *how* and the *when*. When you set your desires, be open to how they may come about, when they may arrive (it could be sooner than you think!), and what they may look like. You'll always get what you genuinely want in the end; it just might look different or happen in a different way than you thought it would. That's because the Universe knows best! Trust it.

✳ DO TAKE INSPIRED ACTION

Manifesting is a process of *co*-creation, meaning you help the Universe create things energetically (with your thoughts and emotions) and physically (with your actions). Contrary to popular belief, most of your manifestations won't simply arrive at your doorstep just because you asked nicely. What's more likely is that you'll ask, and then the Universe will respond by sending you the next step, opportunity, or inspired impulse. Take action on these things! Let the Universe help create *for* you and *through* you.

✳ DO GIVE THANKS IN ADVANCE

Gratitude is beneficial for a few reasons. First of all, it feels good and will help raise your vibration when it is genuine. The second reason is that everyone likes to be thanked, including the Universe! Who do you get more excited to give presents to—the people who couldn't care less or the people who go out of their way to thank you? The appreciative people! So be one of those people. And it's impossible not to manifest things to be grateful for when you're already feeling grateful. That's the Law of Attraction at its finest.

✳ DO HAVE A LITTLE FAITH

Even if you don't know how it can happen, if you can dream it, you can have it. You wouldn't even think the desire if it wasn't already in your energetic realm of possibilities. Trust this and trust that the Universe is much more resourced than you. It literally has everything and everyone at Its disposal to help in the creation of your dream. It also knows the fastest and most efficient ways to make it happen for you—ways you don't even know are possible or available. Have a little faith and trust that if you want it, the Universe can and will do everything to make it happen.

✳ DO IDENTIFY AND ADDRESS ANY RESISTANCE

When things aren't manifesting, it's because we are carrying some form of resistance. Being in resistance means you're practicing split energy. Maybe you want something, but your current vibe is making you a match to something else. Maybe you want something, but certain *parts* of you don't. Or maybe you want something, but your limiting beliefs are stopping you from going for it. These are just a few common ways that resistance can be present within you and sabotage your manifesting efforts without your even knowing it. That's why the brainstorming sessions before each letter in Part 2 give you a chance to ask yourself important questions like, "Is there any part of me that doesn't want this?" and,

"What negative things do I secretly believe may happen if I get what I want?" and, "What limiting beliefs do I have around this topic or desire?"

✳ DO ENJOY THE WAIT

Things can take time to manifest for many valid reasons. Although we are powerful multidimensional beings, we are also humans who live in a 3-D reality. Energies don't always move as quickly as we would like on this plane of existence. So learn how to enjoy the wait! Once you ask, consider it given, and then move on with your life. If you knew for certain that your manifestation was on the way to you and it was only a matter of time, how would you spend the rest of your day, week, month, and year? What enjoyable things would you do to pass the time? Do these things! They will help you release resistance to the present moment.

✳ DON'T FORCE IT

If you're not feeling it, don't force yourself to write a letter to try to manifest in that exact moment. It's not effective to manifest from a place of lack, frustration, impatience, desperation, or anything similar in vibration. When you're feeling like this, which is totally fine, it's your chance to sift through the contrast and get clear about what you want. It's not necessarily the best time to try to manifest something right away. If it feels like you're putting in a lot of effort, try again later, when you're feeling better. It's always more effective to simply wait until you're in alignment.

✳ DON'T JUDGE YOUR DESIRES

When you criticize your desire, it's usually an attempt to un-want it because a part of you just doesn't know how you can ever get it. But you can't un-want what you want! It's literally impossible, because it defies the expansion of the Universe. If you want it, the Universe wants it for you. If you want it, there's always a good reason why. If you want it, you owe it to yourself to at least try to get it.

✳ DON'T BE IMPATIENT, NEEDY, OR RUDE

Nobody likes to be pushed around, and the Universe is no exception. Cultivate patience so you can manifest from a place of play instead of desperation. Resource yourself with what you need so you don't have to beg the Universe in anguish. Be understanding in your interactions with the Universe. A little bit of relaxation and good manners go a long way.

✳ DON'T LIMIT THE UNIVERSE

Surprisingly, when it comes to manifesting, there is such a thing as being *too* specific. Telling the Universe what *kind* of person you want to marry is great, but telling it exactly *who* it has to be is limiting. Now the Universe can't resource all your other potential soul mates! Telling the Universe you want millions of dollars is a good goal, but telling it to send you exactly $1 million is limiting; what if you could have had $10 million? Be specific with how you want to *feel* and the general *flavor* of your creations, but stay open to something better. Again, the Universe knows best. There's no need to micromanage.

TAKING THE NEXT STEP

Now that you've explored the fundamentals of manifestation, it's time to put your new knowledge to the test and work some manifesting magic! In Part 2 of this book, you'll be doing some enlightening self-inquiry and fun intention-setting work for your desires. As tempting as it may be to skip the brainstorming questions and go straight to your letters, your manifesting efforts will go a lot farther if you take the time to reflect on these questions. For guidance in brainstorming and writing your own letters, be sure to check out the example brainstorming session and letter. It's also helpful to meditate before or after you write your letter to help you release resistance, visualize your desire, or gain more clarity and insight.

PART 2

Your Letters

BRAINSTORMING
QUESTIONS
EXAMPLES

WHAT DO I WANT TO MANIFEST?

Don't be shy. All genuine desires are welcome and valid here!

EXAMPLES:

+ I want to be a bestselling author.
+ I want to be pain-free.
+ I want to meet my soul mate soon!
+ I want to experience more ease in my life.
+ I want to own my own home.

WHY DO I WANT IT?

Hint: Think about a feeling. You'll know the answer to this question when you can complete this sentence:
"When I have _____ , I will feel _____ ."

EXAMPLES:

+ I want to start a podcast so I can feel expressive, creative, and connected to cool people.
+ When I have my new luxury electric car, I will feel bougie, baller, and eco-friendly!
+ I want to meet my soul mate so I can feel the amazing experiences of love, romance, partnership, and true compatibility.

WHAT CAN I START DOING *NOW* TO HELP CULTIVATE THIS FEELING IN THE PRESENT?

Once you know how you want to feel, it's time to get creative and think of as many ways as possible to start cultivating these feelings now. What can you add to your daily life to help you feel more of how you want to feel? Make a list!

EXAMPLE: In order to feel more confident, I can...

+ Practice new skills.

+ Give myself compliments.

+ Ask my friends and family what I'm good at.

+ Make a list of all the reasons why I'm valuable.

WHAT AM I WILLING TO *STOP* DOING OR *LET GO OF* TO HELP MAKE MY DREAM A REALITY?

Think about what is holding you back. Are you willing to stop indulging in habits that are keeping you from getting what you want? What are you willing to let go of in order to assist in the creation of your desire?

EXAMPLES:

+ I'm willing to quit the job that I hate.

+ I'm willing to let go of unsupportive people in my life.

+ I'm willing to stop smoking.

+ I'm willing to let go of the fear of failure.

WHAT ARE MY LIMITING BELIEFS RELATIVE TO THIS DESIRE?

What stories do you tell yourself that make it harder for you to have what you want? Bringing these into the light will help you release some resistance. As you realize them,

*have compassion and understanding for the part of you that
learned or created each belief. They didn't come from nowhere!*

EXAMPLES:

✦ Money doesn't grow on trees.

✦ Love never works out for me.

✦ That only happens to lucky people.

WHAT WOULD I RATHER BELIEVE INSTEAD?

*Transform your negative beliefs into empowering narratives and
then look for supportive evidence that makes the new belief seem truer
than the old belief. Pro tip: Finding three or four pieces of supporting
evidence will make it almost impossible not to adopt the new belief.*

EXAMPLES:

✦ Technically, money kind of does grow on trees and it is
everywhere.

✦ Love can work out for me; Just because it didn't before
doesn't mean it can't now. It worked for _____,
_____ , _____ , and _____.

✦ Why not me? If "lucky" people can do it, I can too.

WHAT WILL MY LIFE BE AND FEEL LIKE WHEN I HAVE WHAT I WANT?

*The juicier the details, the better. Get descriptive as you live
in your fulfilled wish and experience your future with your
mind. Use lots of feeling words as you script this out.*

EXAMPLES:

✦ I am so happy to experience _____.

✦ I am relieved to experience _____.

✦ I love _____ about my life.

WHAT ARE FOUR OR FIVE REASONS WHY I CAN AND SHOULD GET WHAT I WANT?

*Remind yourself why you're worthy and capable.
Give yourself a mini pep talk!*

EXAMPLES:

✦ I should go for it while I can, because life is short.

✦ I deserve to be happy just like everyone else.

✦ I'll have so much fun with this.

✦ I'll appreciate it every day.

WHAT SIGNS WILL THE UNIVERSE SHOW ME SO THAT I'LL KNOW MY DESIRE IS ON ITS WAY?

Assign something specific and unique as a secret code the Universe can use to communicate with you. Every time you see that thing, it will be a sign to keep going; your dreams are becoming manifest!

EXAMPLES:

✦ Every time I see a baby bird, I'll know my desire is on its way.

✦ Every time I see the number 1234, I'll know my desire is on its way.

✦ Every time I see something tie-dyed, I'll know my desire is on its way.

WHAT AM I THANKFUL IN ADVANCE FOR?

Raise your vibration by giving thanks in advance for your new future reality.

EXAMPLES:

✦ Thanks in advance for all these blessings...

✦ Thank you, Universe, for these things to come...

A LETTER TO THE UNIVERSE

EXAMPLE

Dear Universe,

I am ready to experience financial freedom! I want to embrace my truly abundant nature and tap in to my personal flow of wealth like never before. I would love to be able to do whatever I want, whenever I want! Being able to have my time back is the freedom that I crave. I know I'll feel so free, generous, comfortable, secure, and grateful when financial freedom is my new normal. I can do so much good in the world and have even more fun in my life when I'm infinitely financially resourced.

I love daydreaming about all the great things I can do with my money! I can see myself now: enjoying my morning coffee on the balcony of my beach home, the sun on my face, overlooking the ocean, feeling thankful that I no longer have to go to a 9-to-5 job I don't like. I'm treating all my friends to a fun trip so we can spend quality time together in a beautiful and new setting, leaving a surprise $1,000 tip for the waiter, paying off my parents' mortgage so they don't have to worry, and watching my kids graduate from the best colleges thanks to our family funds. I'm seeing my passive income grow every month with compound interest!

I'm not sure exactly how to achieve this goal yet, but I'm open! Maybe I can start my own business, learn more about investing, or get a financial adviser....What do you think? I promise to follow the impulses you send me, and I'm willing to put in the effort and make the changes necessary to make this happen.

I know I've been entertaining many thoughts of lack in my life, but I'm ready to turn my mindset around and start noticing how abundant my life already is. I've started writing a gratitude list every morning to help myself feel more abundant and shift my thinking.

Thanks in advance, Universe, for helping me line up with this vision!

Sincerely,

me.

BRAINSTORMING
— ★ QUESTIONS ★ —

What do I want to manifest?

....
....
....
....
....
....
....
....

Why do I want it?

....
....
....
....
....
....
....
....

What can I start doing *now* to help cultivate this feeling in the present?

....
....
....
....
....

What am I willing to *stop* doing or *let go of* to help make my dream a reality?

....
....
....
....
....
....
....
....

What are my limiting beliefs relative to this desire?

....

....

....

....

....

....

What would I rather believe instead?

....

....

....

....

....

....

What will my life be and feel like when I have what I want?

....

....

....

....

....

....

....

What are four or five reasons why I can and should get what I want?

....

....

....

....

....

....

....

What signs will the Universe show me so that I'll know my desire is on its way?

....

....

....

....

....

What am I thankful in advance for?

....

....

....

....

....

....

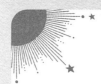

Dear Universe,

....

....

....

....

....

....

....

Thank you, Universe, for...

....

....

....

....

....

....

....

....

....

....

Sincerely,

BRAINSTORMING
★ QUESTIONS ★

What do I want to manifest?

What can I start doing *now* to help cultivate this feeling in the present?

Why do I want it?

What am I willing to *stop* doing or *let go of* to help make my dream a reality?

What are my limiting beliefs relative to this desire?

....

....

....

....

....

What would I rather believe instead?

....

....

....

....

....

....

What will my life be and feel like when I have what I want?

....

....

....

....

....

....

What are four or five reasons why I can and should get what I want?

....

....

....

....

....

....

What signs will the Universe show me so that I'll know my desire is on its way?

....

....

....

....

What am I thankful in advance for?

....

....

....

....

....

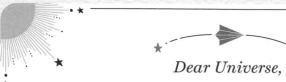

Dear Universe,

....

....

....

....

....

....

....

....

Thank you, Universe, for...

....

....

....

....

....

....

....

....

....

....

Sincerely,

....

BRAINSTORMING
★ QUESTIONS ★

What do I want to manifest?

Why do I want it?

What can I start doing *now* to help cultivate this feeling in the present?

What am I willing to *stop* doing or *let go of* to help make my dream a reality?

What are my limiting beliefs relative to this desire?

....

....

....

....

....

What would I rather believe instead?

....

....

....

....

....

....

What will my life be and feel like when I have what I want?

....

....

....

....

....

....

What are four or five reasons why I can and should get what I want?

....

....

....

....

....

....

What signs will the Universe show me so that I'll know my desire is on its way?

....

....

....

....

What am I thankful in advance for?

....

....

....

....

....

....

Dear Universe,

Thank you, Universe, for...

Sincerely,

BRAINSTORMING
★ QUESTIONS ★

What do I want to manifest?

....
....
....
....
....
....
....
....
....

Why do I want it?

....
....
....
....
....
....
....
....
....

What can I start doing *now* to help cultivate this feeling in the present?

....
....
....
....
....
....
....

What am I willing to *stop* doing or *let go of* to help make my dream a reality?

....
....
....
....
....
....
....
....
....
....

What are my limiting beliefs relative to this desire?

....

....

....

....

....

What would I rather believe instead?

....

....

....

....

....

What will my life be and feel like when I have what I want?

....

....

....

....

....

....

What are four or five reasons why I can and should get what I want?

....

....

....

....

....

....

What signs will the Universe show me so that I'll know my desire is on its way?

....

....

....

....

What am I thankful in advance for?

....

....

....

....

....

Dear Universe,

Thank you, Universe, for...

Sincerely,

BRAINSTORMING
★ QUESTIONS ★

What do I want to manifest?

....
....
....
....
....
....
....
....

Why do I want it?

....
....
....
....
....
....
....
....
....

What can I start doing *now* to help cultivate this feeling in the present?

....
....
....
....
....
....

What am I willing to *stop* doing or *let go of* to help make my dream a reality?

....
....
....
....
....
....
....
....

What are my limiting beliefs relative to this desire?

....

....

....

....

....

What would I rather believe instead?

....

....

....

....

....

....

What will my life be and feel like when I have what I want?

....

....

....

....

....

....

What are four or five reasons why I can and should get what I want?

....

....

....

....

....

....

What signs will the Universe show me so that I'll know my desire is on its way?

....

....

....

....

What am I thankful in advance for?

....

....

....

....

....

....

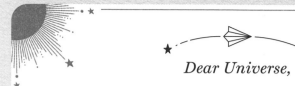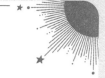

Dear Universe,

....

....

....

....

....

....

....

Thank you, Universe, for...

....

....

....

....

....

....

....

....

....

....

Sincerely,

....

BRAINSTORMING
★ QUESTIONS ★

What do I want to manifest?

....
....
....
....
....
....
....
....

Why do I want it?

....
....
....
....
....
....
....
....

What can I start doing *now* to help cultivate this feeling in the present?

....
....
....
....
....
....
....

What am I willing to *stop* doing or *let go of* to help make my dream a reality?

....
....
....
....
....
....
....
....

What are my limiting beliefs relative to this desire?

....
....
....
....
....
....

What would I rather believe instead?

....
....
....
....
....
....

What will my life be and feel like when I have what I want?

....
....
....
....
....
....

What are four or five reasons why I can and should get what I want?

....
....
....
....
....
....

What signs will the Universe show me so that I'll know my desire is on its way?

....
....
....
....

What am I thankful in advance for?

....
....
....
....
....
....

Dear Universe,

....

....

....

....

....

....

....

....

Thank you, Universe, for...

....

....

....

....

....

....

....

....

....

....

Sincerely,

....

BRAINSTORMING
★ QUESTIONS ★

What do I want to manifest?

....
....
....
....
....
....
....
....

Why do I want it?

....
....
....
....
....
....
....
....
....

What can I start doing *now* to help cultivate this feeling in the present?

....
....
....
....
....
....

What am I willing to *stop* doing or *let go of* to help make my dream a reality?

....
....
....
....
....
....
....
....
....

What are my limiting beliefs relative to this desire?

....

....

....

....

....

What would I rather believe instead?

....

....

....

....

....

What will my life be and feel like when I have what I want?

....

....

....

....

....

....

What are four or five reasons why I can and should get what I want?

....

....

....

....

....

....

What signs will the Universe show me so that I'll know my desire is on its way?

....

....

....

What am I thankful in advance for?

....

....

....

....

....

....

Dear Universe,

Thank you, Universe, for...

Sincerely,

BRAINSTORMING
★ QUESTIONS ★

What do I want to manifest?

....
....
....
....
....
....
....
....

Why do I want it?

....
....
....
....
....
....
....
....
....

What can I start doing *now* to help cultivate this feeling in the present?

....
....
....
....
....
....

What am I willing to *stop* doing or *let go of* to help make my dream a reality?

....
....
....
....
....
....
....
....

What are my limiting beliefs relative to this desire?

....
....
....
....
....
....

What would I rather believe instead?

....
....
....
....
....
....

What will my life be and feel like when I have what I want?

....
....
....
....
....
....
....

What are four or five reasons why I can and should get what I want?

....
....
....
....
....
....

What signs will the Universe show me so that I'll know my desire is on its way?

....
....
....
....
....

What am I thankful in advance for?

....
....
....
....
....
....

Dear Universe,

Thank you, Universe, for...

Sincerely,

BRAINSTORMING
★ QUESTIONS ★

What do I want to manifest?

....

....

....

....

....

....

....

Why do I want it?

....

....

....

....

....

....

....

....

What can I start doing *now* to help cultivate this feeling in the present?

....

....

....

....

....

....

What am I willing to *stop* doing or *let go of* to help make my dream a reality?

....

....

....

....

....

....

....

....

What are my limiting beliefs relative to this desire?

....
....
....
....
....
....

What would I rather believe instead?

....
....
....
....
....
....

What will my life be and feel like when I have what I want?

....
....
....
....
....
....
....

What are four or five reasons why I can and should get what I want?

....
....
....
....
....
....
....

What signs will the Universe show me so that I'll know my desire is on its way?

....
....
....
....

What am I thankful in advance for?

....
....
....
....
....

Dear Universe,

....

....

....

....

....

....

....

....

Thank you, Universe, for...

....

....

....

....

....

....

....

....

....

....

Sincerely,

....

BRAINSTORMING
★ QUESTIONS ★

What do I want to manifest?

....
....
....
....
....
....
....

Why do I want it?

....
....
....
....
....
....
....
....

What can I start doing *now* to help cultivate this feeling in the present?

....
....
....
....
....
....

What am I willing to *stop* doing or *let go of* to help make my dream a reality?

....
....
....
....
....
....
....

What are my limiting beliefs relative to this desire?

....
....
....
....
....

What would I rather believe instead?

....
....
....
....
....

What will my life be and feel like when I have what I want?

....
....
....
....
....
....

What are four or five reasons why I can and should get what I want?

....
....
....
....
....
....

What signs will the Universe show me so that I'll know my desire is on its way?

....
....
....
....

What am I thankful in advance for?

....
....
....
....
....
....

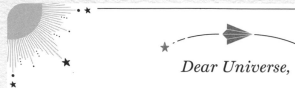

Dear Universe,

....

....

....

....

....

....

....

....

....

....

Thank you, Universe, for...

....

....

....

....

....

....

....

....

....

....

....

....

Sincerely,

....

BRAINSTORMING
★ QUESTIONS ★

What do I want to manifest?

....
....
....
....
....
....
....
....
....

Why do I want it?

....
....
....
....
....
....
....
....
....
....
....

What can I start doing *now* to help cultivate this feeling in the present?

....
....
....
....
....
....

What am I willing to *stop* doing or *let go of* to help make my dream a reality?

....
....
....
....
....
....
....
....
....
....
....

What are my limiting beliefs relative to this desire?

....
....
....
....
....
....

What would I rather believe instead?

....
....
....
....
....
....

What will my life be and feel like when I have what I want?

....
....
....
....
....
....
....

What are four or five reasons why I can and should get what I want?

....
....
....
....
....
....
....

What signs will the Universe show me so that I'll know my desire is on its way?

....
....
....
....
....

What am I thankful in advance for?

....
....
....
....
....
....

Dear Universe,

Thank you, Universe, for...

Sincerely,

BRAINSTORMING
★ QUESTIONS ★

What do I want to manifest?

....

....

....

....

....

....

....

Why do I want it?

....

....

....

....

....

....

....

What can I start doing *now* to help cultivate this feeling in the present?

....

....

....

....

....

....

What am I willing to *stop* doing or *let go of* to help make my dream a reality?

....

....

....

....

....

....

....

What are my limiting beliefs relative to this desire?

....

....

....

....

....

....

What would I rather believe instead?

....

....

....

....

....

....

What will my life be and feel like when I have what I want?

....

....

....

....

....

....

What are four or five reasons why I can and should get what I want?

....

....

....

....

....

....

What signs will the Universe show me so that I'll know my desire is on its way?

....

....

....

....

What am I thankful in advance for?

....

....

....

....

....

Dear Universe,

Thank you, Universe, for...

Sincerely,

BRAINSTORMING
★ QUESTIONS ★

What do I want to manifest?

....
....
....
....
....
....
....
....

Why do I want it?

....
....
....
....
....
....
....
....
....

What can I start doing *now* to help cultivate this feeling in the present?

....
....
....
....
....
....
....

What am I willing to *stop* doing or *let go of* to help make my dream a reality?

....
....
....
....
....
....
....
....
....

What are my limiting beliefs relative to this desire?

....
....
....
....
....
....

What would I rather believe instead?

....
....
....
....
....
....

What will my life be and feel like when I have what I want?

....
....
....
....
....
....

What are four or five reasons why I can and should get what I want?

....
....
....
....
....
....
....

What signs will the Universe show me so that I'll know my desire is on its way?

....
....
....
....
....

What am I thankful in advance for?

....
....
....
....
....
....

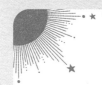

Dear Universe,

Thank you, Universe, for...

Sincerely,

BRAINSTORMING
★ QUESTIONS ★

What do I want to manifest?

....
....
....
....
....
....
....
....

Why do I want it?

....
....
....
....
....
....
....
....
....

What can I start doing *now* to help cultivate this feeling in the present?

....
....
....
....
....
....
....

What am I willing to *stop* doing or *let go of* to help make my dream a reality?

....
....
....
....
....
....
....
....
....

What are my limiting beliefs relative to this desire?

....
....
....
....
....

What would I rather believe instead?

....
....
....
....
....
....

What will my life be and feel like when I have what I want?

....
....
....
....
....
....

What are four or five reasons why I can and should get what I want?

....
....
....
....
....
....
....

What signs will the Universe show me so that I'll know my desire is on its way?

....
....
....
....

What am I thankful in advance for?

....
....
....
....
....
....

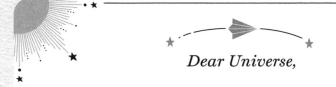

Dear Universe,

Thank you, Universe, for...

Sincerely,

BRAINSTORMING
★ QUESTIONS ★

What do I want to manifest?

....
....
....
....
....
....
....
....

Why do I want it?

....
....
....
....
....
....
....
....
....

What can I start doing *now* to help cultivate this feeling in the present?

....
....
....
....
....
....

What am I willing to *stop* doing or *let go of* to help make my dream a reality?

....
....
....
....
....
....
....
....
....

What are my limiting beliefs relative to this desire?

....
....
....
....
....

What would I rather believe instead?

....
....
....
....
....

What will my life be and feel like when I have what I want?

....
....
....
....
....

What are four or five reasons why I can and should get what I want?

....
....
....
....
....
....

What signs will the Universe show me so that I'll know my desire is on its way?

....
....
....
....

What am I thankful in advance for?

....
....
....
....
....

Dear Universe,

Thank you, Universe, for...

Sincerely,

BRAINSTORMING
★ QUESTIONS ★

What do I want to manifest?

....
....
....
....
....
....
....

Why do I want it?

....
....
....
....
....
....
....
....

What can I start doing *now* to help cultivate this feeling in the present?

....
....
....
....
....
....

What am I willing to *stop* doing or *let go of* to help make my dream a reality?

....
....
....
....
....
....
....
....

What are my limiting beliefs relative to this desire?

....

....

....

....

....

What would I rather believe instead?

....

....

....

....

....

What will my life be and feel like when I have what I want?

....

....

....

....

....

....

What are four or five reasons why I can and should get what I want?

....

....

....

....

....

....

What signs will the Universe show me so that I'll know my desire is on its way?

....

....

....

....

What am I thankful in advance for?

....

....

....

....

....

Dear Universe,

Thank you, Universe, for...

Sincerely,

BRAINSTORMING
★ QUESTIONS ★

What do I want to manifest?

....
....
....
....
....
....
....
....

Why do I want it?

....
....
....
....
....
....
....
....
....

What can I start doing *now* to help cultivate this feeling in the present?

....
....
....
....
....
....

What am I willing to *stop* doing or *let go of* to help make my dream a reality?

....
....
....
....
....
....
....
....
....

What are my limiting beliefs relative to this desire?

....
....
....
....
....
....

What would I rather believe instead?

....
....
....
....
....
....

What will my life be and feel like when I have what I want?

....
....
....
....
....
....
....

What are four or five reasons why I can and should get what I want?

....
....
....
....
....
....
....

What signs will the Universe show me so that I'll know my desire is on its way?

....
....
....
....

What am I thankful in advance for?

....
....
....
....
....
....

Dear Universe,

....

....

....

....

....

....

....

....

Thank you, Universe, for...

....

....

....

....

....

....

....

....

....

....

Sincerely,

....

BRAINSTORMING
★ QUESTIONS ★

What do I want to manifest?

....
....
....
....
....
....
....
....

Why do I want it?

....
....
....
....
....
....
....
....
....

What can I start doing *now* to help cultivate this feeling in the present?

....
....
....
....
....
....
....

What am I willing to *stop* doing or *let go of* to help make my dream a reality?

....
....
....
....
....
....
....
....

What are my limiting beliefs relative to this desire?

....
....
....
....
....

What would I rather believe instead?

....
....
....
....
....

What will my life be and feel like when I have what I want?

....
....
....
....
....
....

What are four or five reasons why I can and should get what I want?

....
....
....
....
....
....

What signs will the Universe show me so that I'll know my desire is on its way?

....
....
....
....

What am I thankful in advance for?

....
....
....
....
....
....

Dear Universe,

....

....

....

....

....

....

....

....

....

Thank you, Universe, for...

....

....

....

....

....

....

....

....

....

....

....

Sincerely,

BRAINSTORMING
★ QUESTIONS ★

What do I want to manifest?

....
....
....
....
....
....
....
....

Why do I want it?

....
....
....
....
....
....
....
....
....

What can I start doing *now* to help cultivate this feeling in the present?

....
....
....
....
....
....
....

What am I willing to *stop* doing or *let go of* to help make my dream a reality?

....
....
....
....
....
....
....
....

What are my limiting beliefs relative to this desire?

....
....
....
....
....
....

What would I rather believe instead?

....
....
....
....
....
....

What will my life be and feel like when I have what I want?

....
....
....
....
....
....

What are four or five reasons why I can and should get what I want?

....
....
....
....
....
....
....

What signs will the Universe show me so that I'll know my desire is on its way?

....
....
....
....

What am I thankful in advance for?

....
....
....
....
....
....

Dear Universe,

Thank you, Universe, for...

Sincerely,

BRAINSTORMING
★ QUESTIONS ★

What do I want to manifest?

....
....
....
....
....
....
....
....

Why do I want it?

....
....
....
....
....
....
....
....
....

What can I start doing *now* to help cultivate this feeling in the present?

....
....
....
....
....
....
....

What am I willing to *stop* doing or *let go of* to help make my dream a reality?

....
....
....
....
....
....
....
....
....

What are my limiting beliefs relative to this desire?

....
....
....
....
....
....

What would I rather believe instead?

....
....
....
....
....
....

What will my life be and feel like when I have what I want?

....
....
....
....
....

What are four or five reasons why I can and should get what I want?

....
....
....
....
....
....
....

What signs will the Universe show me so that I'll know my desire is on its way?

....
....
....
....
....

What am I thankful in advance for?

....
....
....
....
....

Dear Universe,

Thank you, Universe, for...

Sincerely,

BRAINSTORMING
★ QUESTIONS ★

What do I want to manifest?

....
....
....
....
....
....
....
....

Why do I want it?

....
....
....
....
....
....
....
....

What can I start doing *now* to help cultivate this feeling in the present?

....
....
....
....
....
....

What am I willing to *stop* doing or *let go of* to help make my dream a reality?

....
....
....
....
....
....
....
....
....

What are my limiting beliefs relative to this desire?

....
....
....
....
....

What would I rather believe instead?

....
....
....
....
....

What will my life be and feel like when I have what I want?

....
....
....
....
....
....
....

What are four or five reasons why I can and should get what I want?

....
....
....
....
....
....

What signs will the Universe show me so that I'll know my desire is on its way?

....
....
....
....

What am I thankful in advance for?

....
....
....
....
....

Dear Universe,

Thank you, Universe, for...

Sincerely,

BRAINSTORMING
★ QUESTIONS ★

What do I want to manifest?

....
....
....
....
....
....
....
....

Why do I want it?

....
....
....
....
....
....
....
....

What can I start doing *now* to help cultivate this feeling in the present?

....
....
....
....
....
....
....

What am I willing to *stop* doing or *let go of* to help make my dream a reality?

....
....
....
....
....
....
....
....
....

What are my limiting beliefs relative to this desire?

....

....

....

....

....

What would I rather believe instead?

....

....

....

....

....

....

What will my life be and feel like when I have what I want?

....

....

....

....

....

What are four or five reasons why I can and should get what I want?

....

....

....

....

....

....

What signs will the Universe show me so that I'll know my desire is on its way?

....

....

....

....

What am I thankful in advance for?

....

....

....

....

....

Dear Universe,

Thank you, Universe, for...

Sincerely,

BRAINSTORMING
★ QUESTIONS ★

What do I want to manifest?

....
....
....
....
....
....
....
....
....

Why do I want it?

....
....
....
....
....
....
....
....
....

What can I start doing *now* to help cultivate this feeling in the present?

....
....
....
....
....
....

What am I willing to *stop* doing or *let go of* to help make my dream a reality?

....
....
....
....
....
....
....
....
....

What are my limiting beliefs relative to this desire?

....
....
....
....
....
....

What would I rather believe instead?

....
....
....
....
....
....

What will my life be and feel like when I have what I want?

....
....
....
....
....
....
....

What are four or five reasons why I can and should get what I want?

....
....
....
....
....
....

What signs will the Universe show me so that I'll know my desire is on its way?

....
....
....
....

What am I thankful in advance for?

....
....
....
....
....
....
....

Dear Universe,

Thank you, Universe, for...

Sincerely,

BRAINSTORMING
★ QUESTIONS ★

What do I want to manifest?

....
....
....
....
....
....
....

Why do I want it?

....
....
....
....
....
....
....
....
....
....

What can I start doing *now* to help cultivate this feeling in the present?

....
....
....
....
....
....

What am I willing to *stop* doing or *let go of* to help make my dream a reality?

....
....
....
....
....
....
....
....

What are my limiting beliefs relative to this desire?

....

....

....

....

....

What would I rather believe instead?

....

....

....

....

....

What will my life be and feel like when I have what I want?

....

....

....

....

....

....

What are four or five reasons why I can and should get what I want?

....

....

....

....

....

....

What signs will the Universe show me so that I'll know my desire is on its way?

....

....

....

....

What am I thankful in advance for?

....

....

....

....

....

....

Dear Universe,

Thank you, Universe, for...

Sincerely,

BRAINSTORMING
★ QUESTIONS ★

What do I want to manifest?

....
....
....
....
....
....
....

Why do I want it?

....
....
....
....
....
....
....
....
....

What can I start doing *now* to help cultivate this feeling in the present?

....
....
....
....
....
....
....

What am I willing to *stop* doing or *let go of* to help make my dream a reality?

....
....
....
....
....
....
....
....

What are my limiting beliefs relative to this desire?

....

....

....

....

....

What would I rather believe instead?

....

....

....

....

....

What will my life be and feel like when I have what I want?

....

....

....

....

....

....

....

What are four or five reasons why I can and should get what I want?

....

....

....

....

....

What signs will the Universe show me so that I'll know my desire is on its way?

....

....

....

....

What am I thankful in advance for?

....

....

....

....

....

....

Dear Universe,

_____

_____

_____

_____

_____

_____

_____

_____

_____

_____

Thank you, Universe, for...

_____

_____

_____

_____

_____

_____

_____

_____

_____

_____

_____

_____

Sincerely,

_____

BRAINSTORMING
★ QUESTIONS ★

What do I want to manifest?

....
....
....
....
....
....
....
....

Why do I want it?

....
....
....
....
....
....
....
....
....
....

What can I start doing *now* to help cultivate this feeling in the present?

....
....
....
....
....
....
....

What am I willing to *stop* doing or *let go of* to help make my dream a reality?

....
....
....
....
....
....
....
....
....

What are my limiting beliefs relative to this desire?

....

....

....

....

....

What would I rather believe instead?

....

....

....

....

....

....

What will my life be and feel like when I have what I want?

....

....

....

....

....

....

What are four or five reasons why I can and should get what I want?

....

....

....

....

....

....

What signs will the Universe show me so that I'll know my desire is on its way?

....

....

....

....

What am I thankful in advance for?

....

....

....

....

....

....

Dear Universe,

Thank you, Universe, for...

Sincerely,

BRAINSTORMING
★ QUESTIONS ★

What do I want to manifest?

....
....
....
....
....
....
....

Why do I want it?

....
....
....
....
....
....
....
....

What can I start doing *now* to help cultivate this feeling in the present?

....
....
....
....
....
....

What am I willing to *stop* doing or *let go of* to help make my dream a reality?

....
....
....
....
....
....
....
....
....

What are my limiting beliefs relative to this desire?

....
....
....
....
....

What would I rather believe instead?

....
....
....
....
....
....

What will my life be and feel like when I have what I want?

....
....
....
....
....
....

What are four or five reasons why I can and should get what I want?

....
....
....
....
....
....
....

What signs will the Universe show me so that I'll know my desire is on its way?

....
....
....
....

What am I thankful in advance for?

....
....
....
....
....
....

Dear Universe,

Thank you, Universe, for...

Sincerely,

BRAINSTORMING
★ QUESTIONS ★

What do I want to manifest?

....
....
....
....
....
....
....
....
....

Why do I want it?

....
....
....
....
....
....
....
....

What can I start doing *now* to help cultivate this feeling in the present?

....
....
....
....
....
....
....

What am I willing to *stop* doing or *let go of* to help make my dream a reality?

....
....
....
....
....
....
....
....
....

Thank you, Universe, for...

Sincerely,

BRAINSTORMING
★ QUESTIONS ★

What do I want to manifest?

....

....

....

....

....

....

....

Why do I want it?

....

....

....

....

....

....

....

What can I start doing *now* to help cultivate this feeling in the present?

....

....

....

....

....

....

What am I willing to *stop* doing or *let go of* to help make my dream a reality?

....

....

....

....

....

....

....

What are my limiting beliefs relative to this desire?

....
....
....
....
....

What would I rather believe instead?

....
....
....
....
....

What will my life be and feel like when I have what I want?

....
....
....
....
....
....

What are four or five reasons why I can and should get what I want?

....
....
....
....
....
....

What signs will the Universe show me so that I'll know my desire is on its way?

....
....
....
....

What am I thankful in advance for?

....
....
....
....
....

Dear Universe,

Thank you, Universe, for...

Sincerely,

BRAINSTORMING
★ QUESTIONS ★

What do I want to manifest?

....
....
....
....
....
....
....
....
....

Why do I want it?

....
....
....
....
....
....
....
....
....

What can I start doing *now* to help cultivate this feeling in the present?

....
....
....
....
....
....
....

What am I willing to *stop* doing or *let go of* to help make my dream a reality?

....
....
....
....
....
....
....
....
....

What are my limiting beliefs relative
to this desire?

....

....

....

....

....

....

What would I rather believe instead?

....

....

....

....

....

....

What will my life be and feel like
when I have what I want?

....

....

....

....

....

....

What are four or five reasons why I
can and should get what I want?

....

....

....

....

....

....

....

What signs will the Universe show
me so that I'll know my desire is on
its way?

....

....

....

....

What am I thankful in advance for?

....

....

....

....

....

....

Dear Universe,

Thank you, Universe, for...

Sincerely,

BRAINSTORMING
★ QUESTIONS ★

What do I want to manifest?

Why do I want it?

What can I start doing *now* to help cultivate this feeling in the present?

What am I willing to *stop* doing or *let go of* to help make my dream a reality?

What are my limiting beliefs relative to this desire?

....
....
....
....
....
....

What would I rather believe instead?

....
....
....
....
....
....

What will my life be and feel like when I have what I want?

....
....
....
....
....
....
....

What are four or five reasons why I can and should get what I want?

....
....
....
....
....
....
....

What signs will the Universe show me so that I'll know my desire is on its way?

....
....
....
....

What am I thankful in advance for?

....
....
....
....
....
....

Dear Universe,

....

....

....

....

....

....

....

....

Thank you, Universe, for...

....

....

....

....

....

....

....

....

....

....

Sincerely,

....

BRAINSTORMING
★ QUESTIONS ★

What do I want to manifest?

....
....
....
....
....
....
....
....

Why do I want it?

....
....
....
....
....
....
....
....
....
....

What can I start doing *now* to help cultivate this feeling in the present?

....
....
....
....
....
....

What am I willing to *stop* doing or *let go of* to help make my dream a reality?

....
....
....
....
....
....
....
....
....
....

What are my limiting beliefs relative to this desire?

....
....
....
....
....

What would I rather believe instead?

....
....
....
....
....
....

What will my life be and feel like when I have what I want?

....
....
....
....
....
....

What are four or five reasons why I can and should get what I want?

....
....
....
....
....
....

What signs will the Universe show me so that I'll know my desire is on its way?

....
....
....
....

What am I thankful in advance for?

....
....
....
....
....
....

Dear Universe,

Thank you, Universe, for...

Sincerely,

BRAINSTORMING
★ QUESTIONS ★

What do I want to manifest?

....
....
....
....
....
....
....
....

Why do I want it?

....
....
....
....
....
....
....
....
....

What can I start doing *now* to help cultivate this feeling in the present?

....
....
....
....
....
....

What am I willing to *stop* doing or *let go of* to help make my dream a reality?

....
....
....
....
....
....
....
....
....

What are my limiting beliefs relative to this desire?

....
....
....
....
....

What would I rather believe instead?

....
....
....
....
....
....
....

What will my life be and feel like when I have what I want?

....
....
....
....
....
....
....

What are four or five reasons why I can and should get what I want?

....
....
....
....
....
....
....

What signs will the Universe show me so that I'll know my desire is on its way?

....
....
....
....

What am I thankful in advance for?

....
....
....
....
....
....

Dear Universe,

Thank you, Universe, for...

Sincerely,

BRAINSTORMING
★ QUESTIONS ★

What do I want to manifest?

....
....
....
....
....
....
....

Why do I want it?

....
....
....
....
....
....
....

What can I start doing *now* to help cultivate this feeling in the present?

....
....
....
....
....
....

What am I willing to *stop* doing or *let go of* to help make my dream a reality?

....
....
....
....
....
....
....

What are my limiting beliefs relative to this desire?

....

....

....

....

....

What would I rather believe instead?

....

....

....

....

....

What will my life be and feel like when I have what I want?

....

....

....

....

....

....

What are four or five reasons why I can and should get what I want?

....

....

....

....

....

....

What signs will the Universe show me so that I'll know my desire is on its way?

....

....

....

....

What am I thankful in advance for?

....

....

....

....

....

....

Dear Universe,

Thank you, Universe, for...

Sincerely,

BRAINSTORMING
★ QUESTIONS ★

What do I want to manifest?

....
....
....
....
....
....
....
....

Why do I want it?

....
....
....
....
....
....
....
....

What can I start doing *now* to help cultivate this feeling in the present?

....
....
....
....
....
....
....

What am I willing to *stop* doing or *let go of* to help make my dream a reality?

....
....
....
....
....
....
....
....

What are my limiting beliefs relative to this desire?

....
....
....
....
....

What would I rather believe instead?

....
....
....
....
....

What will my life be and feel like when I have what I want?

....
....
....
....
....
....

What are four or five reasons why I can and should get what I want?

....
....
....
....
....
....

What signs will the Universe show me so that I'll know my desire is on its way?

....
....
....
....

What am I thankful in advance for?

....
....
....
....
....
....

Dear Universe,

....

....

....

....

....

....

....

....

Thank you, Universe, for...

....

....

....

....

....

....

....

....

....

....

....

Sincerely,

....

BRAINSTORMING
★ QUESTIONS ★

What do I want to manifest?

....
....
....
....
....
....
....
....

Why do I want it?

....
....
....
....
....
....
....
....

What can I start doing *now* to help cultivate this feeling in the present?

....
....
....
....
....
....
....

What am I willing to *stop* doing or *let go of* to help make my dream a reality?

....
....
....
....
....
....
....
....

What are my limiting beliefs relative to this desire?

....

....

....

....

....

....

What would I rather believe instead?

....

....

....

....

....

....

What will my life be and feel like when I have what I want?

....

....

....

....

....

....

What are four or five reasons why I can and should get what I want?

....

....

....

....

....

....

....

What signs will the Universe show me so that I'll know my desire is on its way?

....

....

....

....

What am I thankful in advance for?

....

....

....

....

....

....

Dear Universe,

Thank you, Universe, for...

Sincerely,

BRAINSTORMING
★ QUESTIONS ★

What do I want to manifest?

....
....
....
....
....
....
....
....

Why do I want it?

....
....
....
....
....
....
....
....
....
....

What can I start doing *now* to help cultivate this feeling in the present?

....
....
....
....
....
....
....

What am I willing to *stop* doing or *let go of* to help make my dream a reality?

....
....
....
....
....
....
....
....
....

What are my limiting beliefs relative to this desire?

....

....

....

....

....

....

What would I rather believe instead?

....

....

....

....

....

....

....

What will my life be and feel like when I have what I want?

....

....

....

....

....

....

What are four or five reasons why I can and should get what I want?

....

....

....

....

....

....

....

What signs will the Universe show me so that I'll know my desire is on its way?

....

....

....

....

....

What am I thankful in advance for?

....

....

....

....

....

....

Dear Universe,

....
....
....
....
....
....
....
....
....
....
....
....
....
....
....
....
....
....
....
....
....
....
....

Thank you, Universe, for...

Sincerely,

BRAINSTORMING
★ QUESTIONS ★

What do I want to manifest?

....
....
....
....
....
....
....
....

Why do I want it?

....
....
....
....
....
....
....
....
....

What can I start doing *now* to help cultivate this feeling in the present?

....
....
....
....
....
....
....

What am I willing to *stop* doing or *let go of* to help make my dream a reality?

....
....
....
....
....
....
....
....
....
....

What are my limiting beliefs relative to this desire?

....
....
....
....
....
....

What would I rather believe instead?

....
....
....
....
....
....

What will my life be and feel like when I have what I want?

....
....
....
....
....
....
....

What are four or five reasons why I can and should get what I want?

....
....
....
....
....
....
....
....

What signs will the Universe show me so that I'll know my desire is on its way?

....
....
....
....
....

What am I thankful in advance for?

....
....
....
....
....
....

Dear Universe,

....

....

....

....

....

....

....

....

Thank you, Universe, for...

....

....

....

....

....

....

....

....

....

....

....

Sincerely,

....

BRAINSTORMING
★ QUESTIONS ★

What do I want to manifest?

....
....
....
....
....
....
....
....
....

Why do I want it?

....
....
....
....
....
....
....
....
....

What can I start doing *now* to help cultivate this feeling in the present?

....
....
....
....
....
....
....

What am I willing to *stop* doing or *let go of* to help make my dream a reality?

....
....
....
....
....
....
....
....
....

What are my limiting beliefs relative to this desire?

....

....

....

....

....

What would I rather believe instead?

....

....

....

....

....

....

What will my life be and feel like when I have what I want?

....

....

....

....

....

....

What are four or five reasons why I can and should get what I want?

....

....

....

....

....

....

What signs will the Universe show me so that I'll know my desire is on its way?

....

....

....

....

What am I thankful in advance for?

....

....

....

....

....

Dear Universe,

Thank you, Universe, for...

Sincerely,

BRAINSTORMING
★ QUESTIONS ★

What do I want to manifest?

....

....

....

....

....

....

....

....

....

....

Why do I want it?

....

....

....

....

....

....

....

....

....

....

....

What can I start doing *now* to help cultivate this feeling in the present?

....

....

....

....

....

....

....

....

What am I willing to *stop* doing or *let go of* to help make my dream a reality?

....

....

....

....

....

....

....

....

....

....

What are my limiting beliefs relative to this desire?

....

....

....

....

....

What would I rather believe instead?

....

....

....

....

....

....

What will my life be and feel like when I have what I want?

....

....

....

....

....

....

What are four or five reasons why I can and should get what I want?

....

....

....

....

....

....

What signs will the Universe show me so that I'll know my desire is on its way?

....

....

....

....

What am I thankful in advance for?

....

....

....

....

....

....

Dear Universe,

Thank you, Universe, for...

Sincerely,

BRAINSTORMING
★ QUESTIONS ★

What do I want to manifest?

....

....

....

....

....

....

....

....

Why do I want it?

....

....

....

....

....

....

....

....

What can I start doing *now* to help cultivate this feeling in the present?

....

....

....

....

....

What am I willing to *stop* doing or *let go of* to help make my dream a reality?

....

....

....

....

....

....

....

....

What are my limiting beliefs relative to this desire?

....

....

....

....

....

....

What would I rather believe instead?

....

....

....

....

....

....

What will my life be and feel like when I have what I want?

....

....

....

....

....

....

....

What are four or five reasons why I can and should get what I want?

....

....

....

....

....

....

....

What signs will the Universe show me so that I'll know my desire is on its way?

....

....

....

....

....

What am I thankful in advance for?

....

....

....

....

....

....

Dear Universe,

Thank you, Universe, for...

Sincerely,

BRAINSTORMING
★ QUESTIONS ★

What do I want to manifest?

....
....
....
....
....
....
....
....

Why do I want it?

....
....
....
....
....
....
....
....
....
....
....

What can I start doing *now* to help cultivate this feeling in the present?

....
....
....
....
....
....
....

What am I willing to *stop* doing or *let go of* to help make my dream a reality?

....
....
....
....
....
....
....
....
....
....

What are my limiting beliefs relative to this desire?

....
....
....
....
....
....

What would I rather believe instead?

....
....
....
....
....
....

What will my life be and feel like when I have what I want?

....
....
....
....
....
....

What are four or five reasons why I can and should get what I want?

....
....
....
....
....
....
....

What signs will the Universe show me so that I'll know my desire is on its way?

....
....
....
....
....

What am I thankful in advance for?

....
....
....
....
....
....

Dear Universe,

Thank you, Universe, for...

Sincerely,

BRAINSTORMING
★ QUESTIONS ★

What do I want to manifest?

....

....

....

....

....

....

....

Why do I want it?

....

....

....

....

....

....

....

What can I start doing *now* to help cultivate this feeling in the present?

....

....

....

....

....

....

What am I willing to *stop* doing or *let go of* to help make my dream a reality?

....

....

....

....

....

....

....

What are my limiting beliefs relative to this desire?

....
....
....
....
....
....

What would I rather believe instead?

....
....
....
....
....
....

What will my life be and feel like when I have what I want?

....
....
....
....
....
....
....

What are four or five reasons why I can and should get what I want?

....
....
....
....
....
....
....

What signs will the Universe show me so that I'll know my desire is on its way?

....
....
....
....

What am I thankful in advance for?

....
....
....
....
....
....

Dear Universe,

Thank you, Universe, for...

Sincerely,

BRAINSTORMING
★ QUESTIONS ★

What do I want to manifest?

....

....

....

....

....

....

....

....

Why do I want it?

....

....

....

....

....

....

....

....

What can I start doing *now* to help cultivate this feeling in the present?

....

....

....

....

....

....

What am I willing to *stop* doing or *let go of* to help make my dream a reality?

....

....

....

....

....

....

....

....

What are my limiting beliefs relative to this desire?

....
....
....
....
....
....

What would I rather believe instead?

....
....
....
....
....
....

What will my life be and feel like when I have what I want?

....
....
....
....
....
....
....

What are four or five reasons why I can and should get what I want?

....
....
....
....
....
....
....

What signs will the Universe show me so that I'll know my desire is on its way?

....
....
....
....
....

What am I thankful in advance for?

....
....
....
....
....

Dear Universe,

Thank you, Universe, for...

Sincerely,

BRAINSTORMING
★ QUESTIONS ★

What do I want to manifest?

....
....
....
....
....
....
....
....

Why do I want it?

....
....
....
....
....
....
....
....

What can I start doing *now* to help cultivate this feeling in the present?

....
....
....
....
....
....

What am I willing to *stop* doing or *let go of* to help make my dream a reality?

....
....
....
....
....
....
....
....

What are my limiting beliefs relative to this desire?

....
....
....
....
....
....

What would I rather believe instead?

....
....
....
....
....
....

What will my life be and feel like when I have what I want?

....
....
....
....
....
....

What are four or five reasons why I can and should get what I want?

....
....
....
....
....
....
....

What signs will the Universe show me so that I'll know my desire is on its way?

....
....
....
....
....

What am I thankful in advance for?

....
....
....
....
....

Dear Universe,

Thank you, Universe, for...

Sincerely,

BRAINSTORMING
★ QUESTIONS ★

What do I want to manifest?

....
....
....
....
....
....
....
....
....

Why do I want it?

....
....
....
....
....
....
....
....
....
....

What can I start doing *now* to help cultivate this feeling in the present?

....
....
....
....
....
....
....

What am I willing to *stop* doing or *let go of* to help make my dream a reality?

....
....
....
....
....
....
....
....
....

What are my limiting beliefs relative to this desire?

....

....

....

....

....

....

What would I rather believe instead?

....

....

....

....

....

....

What will my life be and feel like when I have what I want?

....

....

....

....

....

....

What are four or five reasons why I can and should get what I want?

....

....

....

....

....

....

....

....

What signs will the Universe show me so that I'll know my desire is on its way?

....

....

....

....

What am I thankful in advance for?

....

....

....

....

....

....

Dear Universe,

··
··
··
··
··
··
··
··
··
··
··
··
··
··
··
··
··
··
··
··
··
··
··
··
··
··

Thank you, Universe, for...

Sincerely,

BRAINSTORMING
★ QUESTIONS ★

What do I want to manifest?

....

....

....

....

....

....

....

....

Why do I want it?

....

....

....

....

....

....

....

....

What can I start doing *now* to help cultivate this feeling in the present?

....

....

....

....

....

....

What am I willing to *stop* doing or *let go of* to help make my dream a reality?

....

....

....

....

....

....

....

....

....

What are my limiting beliefs relative to this desire?

....

....

....

....

....

What would I rather believe instead?

....

....

....

....

....

....

What will my life be and feel like when I have what I want?

....

....

....

....

....

....

What are four or five reasons why I can and should get what I want?

....

....

....

....

....

....

....

What signs will the Universe show me so that I'll know my desire is on its way?

....

....

....

....

What am I thankful in advance for?

....

....

....

....

....

....

Dear Universe,

Thank you, Universe, for...

Sincerely,

BRAINSTORMING
★ QUESTIONS ★

What do I want to manifest?

....
....
....
....
....
....
....
....

Why do I want it?

....
....
....
....
....
....
....
....
....

What can I start doing *now* to help cultivate this feeling in the present?

....
....
....
....
....
....

What am I willing to *stop* doing or *let go of* to help make my dream a reality?

....
....
....
....
....
....
....
....
....

What are my limiting beliefs relative to this desire?

....

....

....

....

....

What would I rather believe instead?

....

....

....

....

....

....

What will my life be and feel like when I have what I want?

....

....

....

....

....

What are four or five reasons why I can and should get what I want?

....

....

....

....

....

....

....

What signs will the Universe show me so that I'll know my desire is on its way?

....

....

....

....

What am I thankful in advance for?

....

....

....

....

....

Dear Universe,

Thank you, Universe, for...

Sincerely,

BRAINSTORMING
★ QUESTIONS ★

What do I want to manifest?

....
....
....
....
....
....
....
....

Why do I want it?

....
....
....
....
....
....
....
....
....

What can I start doing *now* to help cultivate this feeling in the present?

....
....
....
....
....
....

What am I willing to *stop* doing or *let go of* to help make my dream a reality?

....
....
....
....
....
....
....
....
....
....

What are my limiting beliefs relative to this desire?

....

....

....

....

....

What would I rather believe instead?

....

....

....

....

....

....

What will my life be and feel like when I have what I want?

....

....

....

....

....

....

....

What are four or five reasons why I can and should get what I want?

....

....

....

....

....

....

....

What signs will the Universe show me so that I'll know my desire is on its way?

....

....

....

....

....

What am I thankful in advance for?

....

....

....

....

....

....

Dear Universe,

Thank you, Universe, for...

Sincerely,

BRAINSTORMING
★ QUESTIONS ★

What do I want to manifest?

....
....
....
....
....
....
....
....

Why do I want it?

....
....
....
....
....
....
....
....

What can I start doing *now* to help cultivate this feeling in the present?

....
....
....
....
....
....
....

What am I willing to *stop* doing or *let go of* to help make my dream a reality?

....
....
....
....
....
....
....
....

What are my limiting beliefs relative to this desire?

....

....

....

....

....

....

What would I rather believe instead?

....

....

....

....

....

....

What will my life be and feel like when I have what I want?

....

....

....

....

....

....

....

What are four or five reasons why I can and should get what I want?

....

....

....

....

....

....

What signs will the Universe show me so that I'll know my desire is on its way?

....

....

....

....

What am I thankful in advance for?

....

....

....

....

....

....

Dear Universe,

Thank you, Universe, for...

Sincerely,

BRAINSTORMING
★ QUESTIONS ★

What do I want to manifest?

....

....

....

....

....

....

....

Why do I want it?

....

....

....

....

....

....

....

What can I start doing *now* to help cultivate this feeling in the present?

....

....

....

....

....

....

....

What am I willing to *stop* doing or *let go of* to help make my dream a reality?

....

....

....

....

....

....

....

What are my limiting beliefs relative to this desire?

....
....
....
....
....
....

What would I rather believe instead?

....
....
....
....
....
....

What will my life be and feel like when I have what I want?

....
....
....
....
....
....
....

What are four or five reasons why I can and should get what I want?

....
....
....
....
....
....
....

What signs will the Universe show me so that I'll know my desire is on its way?

....
....
....
....
....

What am I thankful in advance for?

....
....
....
....
....
....

Dear Universe,

Thank you, Universe, for...

Sincerely,